Creative and Delicious Waffle

Delights

Sweet and Savory Waffles from Around the World

The Perfect Waffle Party

By: Samantha Rich

License Notes

The material presented in this book is the sole intellectual property of the author and is safeguarded by copyright laws. Without written permission from the author, it is strictly prohibited to copy, publish, or distribute any portion or all of the content.

The author has taken great care to ensure the accuracy of the information provided, making it a valuable educational resource. It is the responsibility of the reader to handle the book with care, as the author will not be held responsible for any misuse or resulting consequences.

Table of Contents

Introduction

Is breakfast your preferred morning meal? Tell me about your typical morning meal. A decent waffle is a necessity if you value breakfast. Waffles, a popular breakfast food, are produced by frying leavened batter in a double-sided hot iron grill. Waffles can be created with almost any kind of batter, so it's easy to twist them to suit a wide variety of preferences. Waffles can be sweet or savory, with whipped cream, icing, maple syrup, or meat and gravy as toppings. It's all up to you, and *"Wafflelicious: 30 Creative and Delicious Waffle Delights"* is here to help you explore your wildest waffle desires.

HHHHHHHHHHHHHHHHHHHHHHHHHHHHHH

1. Cranberry Waffles

Duration: 30 minutes

Yield: 12 waffles

Ingredient List

- Egg Replacer (2 tbsp.)
- Hot water (1/4 cup)
- Flour (1 ½ cups)
- Granulated sugar (3/4 cup)
- Baking powder (1 tsp.)
- Baking soda (1/2 tsp.)
- Salt (1/4 tsp.)
- Cranberries (1/2 cup, with sauce)
- Dairy-free soy margarine (1/2 cup, melted)
- Dairy-free soy yogurt (1/2 cup)
- Vanilla extract (1 tsp.)
- Nutmeg (1/2 tsp.)

HHHHHHHHHHHHHHHHHHHHHHHHHHHHHH

How to Cook:

a) Combine all the ingredients listed in the recipe in a large mixing bowl or a stand mixer. Whisk them well until the mixture forms a smooth batter.

b) Allow the batter to rest for about 10 minutes.

c) Preheat the waffle iron according to the manufacturer's instructions.

d) Pour about 1/3 cup of the batter onto the waffle iron and close the lid.

e) Cook the waffle for about 4 minutes or until golden brown. Remove the waffle from the iron and repeat with the remaining batter.

f) Serve and enjoy your delicious waffles!

Cooking Notes:

a) It's important to let the batter rest for a few minutes to allow the ingredients to fully incorporate and produce a better texture.

b) The amount of batter poured onto the waffle iron may vary depending on the size of the iron and personal preference. Adjust accordingly.

c) Make sure to follow the manufacturer's instructions when preheating and using the waffle iron to avoid any accidents.

2. Rum and Raisin Waffles

Duration: 30 minutes

Yield: 12 waffles

Ingredient List

- Egg Replacer (2 tbsp.)
- Hot water (1/4 cup)
- Flour (1 ½ cups)
- Granulated sugar (3/4 cup)
- Baking powder (1 tsp.)
- Baking soda (1/2 tsp.)
- Salt (1/4 tsp.)
- Raisins (1/4 cup)
- Dairy-free soy margarine (1/2 cup, melted)
- Dairy-free soy yogurt (1/2 cup)
- Vanilla extract (1 tsp.)
- Nutmeg (1/2 tsp.)
- Cinnamon (1/2 tsp.)

HHHHHHHHHHHHHHHHHHHHHHHHHHHHHH

How to Cook:

a) Gather all ingredients and necessary equipment, including a large mixing bowl or stand mixer and a waffle iron.

b) Combine all the ingredients in the mixing bowl or stand mixer.

c) Whisk the ingredients together until they are fully combined, and the mixture forms a smooth batter.

d) Allow the batter to rest for 10 minutes to activate the leavening agents and improve the texture of the waffles.

e) Preheat the waffle iron to the desired temperature.

f) Pour 1/3 cup of batter onto the waffle iron and cook for approximately 4 minutes or until the waffle is golden brown.

g) Serve the waffles with your desired toppings, such as butter, syrup, fruit, or whipped cream.

Cooking Notes:

a) It's important to let the batter rest before cooking the waffles. This will give the batter time to thicken and allow the waffles to rise properly.

b) Be sure to preheat the waffle iron to the desired temperature before cooking the waffles.

c) The cooking time may vary depending on the type and temperature of your waffle iron. Check the manufacturer's instructions for recommended cooking times.

3. Pear Waffles

Duration: 30 minutes

Yield: 12 waffles

Ingredient List

- Egg Replacer (2 tbsp.)
- Hot water (1/4 cup)
- Flour (1 ½ cups)
- Granulated sugar (3/4 cup)
- Baking powder (1 tsp.)
- Baking soda (1/2 tsp.)
- Salt (1/4 tsp.)
- Pears (1/2 cup, mashed)
- Pears (1/2 cup, chopped)
- Dairy-free soy margarine (1/2 cup, melted)
- Dairy-free soy yogurt (1/2 cup)
- Vanilla extract (1 tsp.)
- Ginger (1 tsp., ground)
- Nutmeg (1/2 tsp.)

HHHHHHHHHHHHHHHHHHHHHHHHHHHHHH

How to Cook:

a) In a large mixing bowl or stand mixer, combine all the ingredients from the ingredient list.

b) Whisk the mixture until it is fully combined and forms a smooth batter.

c) Let the batter rest for 10 minutes to allow the ingredients to meld together.

d) Preheat the waffle iron.

e) Pour 1/3 cup of batter onto the waffle iron and cook for 4 minutes or until golden brown.

f) Serve the waffles hot and enjoy!

Cooking Notes:

a) Be careful not to overmix the batter, as this can lead to tough waffles. Mix just until the ingredients are combined.

b) Letting the batter rest for 10 minutes allows the gluten in the flour to relax, resulting in a tender waffle.

c) When pouring the batter onto the waffle iron, be careful not to overfill it. This can cause the batter to overflow and create a mess.

d) To keep the waffles warm while cooking the remaining batter, place them in a 200°F (93°C) oven until ready to serve.

4. Blueberry Waffles

Duration: 30 minutes

Yield: 12 waffles

Ingredient List

- Dairy-free soy margarine (3/4 cups, softened)
- Granulated sugar (1 ½ cup)
- Soy yogurt vanilla (1/4 cup)
- Vanilla (2 tsp.)
- Silken tofu (1/4 cup, pureed)
- All-purpose flour (2 cups)
- Baking powder (1 tsp.)
- Salt (1 tsp.)
- Coconut milk (1 cup)
- Blueberries-fresh (1 cup, crushed)

HHHHHHHHHHHHHHHHHHHHHHHHHHHHH

How to Cook:

a) Gather all the ingredients and the necessary kitchen tools such as a mixing bowl, a whisk, and a waffle iron.

b) Combine all the ingredients in the mixing bowl and whisk until the batter is fully combined and smooth.

c) Let the batter rest for 10 minutes to allow the gluten to relax, resulting in a better texture for the waffles.

d) Preheat the waffle iron according to the manufacturer's instructions.

e) Pour 1/3 cup of the batter onto the waffle iron and close the lid. Cook for 4 minutes or until golden brown.

f) Serve the waffles immediately with your choice of toppings, such as maple syrup, whipped cream, fresh fruit, or butter.

Cooking Notes:

a) To prevent the waffles from sticking to the iron, make sure to grease it with cooking spray or butter before pouring the batter.

b) Be careful not to overfill the iron with batter, as it can overflow and make a mess.

c) Waffles are best served immediately after cooking to ensure they remain crisp and fluffy. If you need to keep them warm, place them on a baking sheet in a 200°F oven until ready to serve.

5. Banana-Nut Waffles

Duration: 40 minutes

Yield: 12 waffles

Ingredient List

- Egg Replacer (2 tbsp.)
- Hot water (1/4 cup)
- Flour (1 ½ cups)
- Granulated sugar (3/4 cup)
- Baking powder (1 tsp.)
- Baking soda (1/2 tsp.)
- Salt (1/4 tsp.)
- Almonds (1/4 cup, crushed)
- Peanuts (1/4 cup, crushed)
- Bananas (1 cup, mashed)
- Dairy-free soy margarine (1/2 cup, melted)
- Dairy-free soy yogurt (1/2 cup)
- Vanilla extract (1 tsp.)

HHHHHHHHHHHHHHHHHHHHHHHHHHHH

How to Cook:

a) Combine all the ingredients listed in a large mixing bowl or in a stand mixer.

b) Whisk the mixture until it forms a smooth batter.

c) Let the batter rest for 10 minutes to allow it to thicken and develop flavor.

d) Preheat your waffle iron according to the manufacturer's instructions.

e) Pour 1/3 cup of the batter onto the waffle iron and spread it evenly.

f) Cook the waffle for 4-5 minutes or until golden brown and crispy.

Cooking Notes:

a) You can use a whisk, hand mixer, or stand mixer to combine the ingredients.

b) It's important to let the batter rest for a few minutes to allow the flour to hydrate and the batter to thicken.

c) The cooking time may vary depending on the type of waffle iron you have, so check the manufacturer's instructions for specific details.

6. Coconut Waffles

Duration: 40 minutes

Yield: 16 waffles

Ingredient List

- All-purpose flour (2 cups)
- Baking powder (2 tsp.)
- Salt (1/4 tsp.)
- Coconut (1/2 cup, flaked)
- Dairy-free soy margarine (1 stick, cold)
- Granulated sugar (1 1/3 cup)
- Coconut milk (1 cup)
- Egg Replacer powder (3 tbsp. dissolved in ¼ cup hot water)
- Apple cider vinegar (1 tsp.)

HHHHHHHHHHHHHHHHHHHHHHHHHHHHHH

How to Cook:

a) Combine all the ingredients listed in a large mixing bowl or stand mixer.
b) Whisk the mixture until it forms a smooth batter.
c) Let the batter rest for 10 minutes to allow the ingredients to fully combine.
d) Preheat the waffle iron to the desired temperature.
e) Pour 1/3 cup of the batter onto the preheated waffle iron.
f) Cook the waffle for about 4 minutes or until it is golden brown.
g) Serve and enjoy the delicious waffles!

Cooking Notes:

a) Make sure to preheat the waffle iron before pouring the batter.
b) Depending on your waffle iron, cooking time and temperature may vary.
c) Serve the waffles with your favorite toppings such as maple syrup, fresh fruit, whipped cream, or chocolate chips.

7. Carrot Cake Waffles

Duration: 35 minutes

Yield: 12 waffles

Ingredient List

- Flour (1 ½ cup)
- Baking soda (1 tsp.)
- Ginger (1 tsp, ground)
- Cinnamon (1 tsp.)
- Nutmeg (1/4 tsp)
- Salt (1/2 tsp.)
- Granulated sugar (1 ¼ cup)
- Sugar-brown (1/3 cup)
- Baking powder (1/2 tsp.)
- Canola oil (1/2 cup)
- Soy yogurt (2 tsp., vanilla)
- Vanilla (1 tsp.)
- Carrots (2 cups, shredded)
- Pineapple (1/2 cup, crushed)
- Walnuts (1 cup, chopped)

HHHHHHHHHHHHHHHHHHHHHHHHHHHH

How to Cook:

a) In a large mixing bowl or stand mixer, combine all ingredients listed and whisk until fully combined, and the mixture forms a smooth batter.

b) Let the batter rest for 10 minutes to allow the ingredients to meld together.

c) Preheat the waffle iron.

d) Once the iron is heated, pour 1/3 cup of the batter on the iron.

e) Cook the waffles for 4 minutes or until they are golden brown.

f) Serve the waffles hot and enjoy.

Cooking Notes:

a) If the batter is too thick, you can add a little bit of milk to thin it out.

b) You can keep the cooked waffles warm by placing them in a preheated oven at 200°F until you're ready to serve.

7. Raspberry Waffles

Duration: 30 minutes

Yield: 12 waffles

Ingredient List

- Flour (1 ½ cups)
- Baking powder (1/2 tsp.)
- Extra virgin olive oil (1/3 cup)
- Dairy-free soy margarine (1/2 cup, melted)
- Baking soda (1/2 tsp.)
- Soy milk (1/2 cup)
- Granulated sugar (3/4 cup)
- Raspberries (1/4 cup, chopped)
- Salt (1/4 tsp.)

HHHHHHHHHHHHHHHHHHHHHHHHHHHHHHH

How to Cook:

a) Combine all the ingredients in a large mixing bowl or stand mixer. Whisk until fully combined, and the mixture forms a smooth batter.

b) Let the batter rest for 10 minutes to allow the ingredients to meld together.

c) Preheat the waffle iron to the desired temperature.

d) Once the waffle iron is heated, pour 1/3 cup of batter onto the center of the iron.

e) Close the lid of the waffle iron and cook the waffle for about 4 minutes, or until it is golden brown.

f) Carefully remove the waffle from the iron and serve hot with your favorite toppings, such as syrup, fruit, or whipped cream.

Cooking Notes:

a) Be sure to thoroughly mix the batter until smooth to avoid any lumps in the waffles.

b) Allowing the batter to rest for a few minutes can help the waffles achieve a better texture and rise.

c) The cooking time may vary depending on the type and model of your waffle iron. Check the manufacturer's instructions for best results.

8. Cherry Waffles

Duration: 30 minutes

Yield: 12 waffles

Ingredient List

- Flour (1 ¾ cups)
- Baking powder (1/2 tsp.)
- Extra virgin olive oil (1/3 cup)
- Soy milk (1 cup)
- Granulated sugar (3/4 cup)
- Baking soda (1/2 tsp.)
- Cherries (1/2 cup, pureed)
- Lemon Juice (1 tsp.)
- Salt (1/4 tsp.)

HHHHHHHHHHHHHHHHHHHHHHHHHHHHHH

How to Cook:

a) In a large mixing bowl or stand mixer, combine all the ingredients listed in the recipe.

b) Whisk the mixture until all the ingredients are fully combined and the batter becomes smooth.

c) Let the batter rest for 10 minutes to allow the gluten to relax and the ingredients to fully incorporate.

d) Preheat the waffle iron to the desired temperature according to the manufacturer's instructions.

e) Pour 1/3 cup of the batter onto the waffle iron and spread it evenly.

f) Cook for about 4 minutes or until golden brown and crispy.

g) Serve and enjoy your freshly made waffles with your favorite toppings, such as syrup, butter, fruits, or whipped cream.

Cooking Notes:

a) Be careful not to overmix the batter as it can result in tough waffles.

b) Adjust the waffle iron's temperature and cooking time according to your preference for crispy or soft waffles.

c) You can also add some flavors or textures to the batter, such as chocolate chips, cinnamon, or chopped nuts.

9. Orange Waffles

Duration: 30 minutes

Yield: 12 waffles

Ingredient List

- All-purpose flour (1 ½ cups)
- Orange juice (1/4 cup, freshly squeezed)
- Baking powder (1/2 tsp.)
- Baking soda (1/2 tsp.)
- Extra virgin olive oil (1/3 cup)
- Soy milk (1 cup)
- Granulated sugar (3/4 cup)
- Orange rind (chopped finely)
- Salt (1/4 tsp.)

HHHHHHHHHHHHHHHHHHHHHHHHHHHHHH

How to Cook:

a) Combine all ingredients in a large mixing bowl or stand mixer.

b) Whisk the mixture until it is fully combined and forms a smooth batter.

c) Allow the batter to rest for 10 minutes.

d) Preheat the waffle iron.

e) Pour 1/3 cup of the batter onto the iron.

f) Cook the waffle for 4 minutes or until golden brown.

g) Serve and enjoy.

Cooking Notes:

a) Make sure to not overmix the batter as it can lead to tough waffles.

b) Letting the batter rest allows the gluten to relax, resulting in a lighter and fluffier waffle.

c) Adjust the cooking time according to your waffle iron's instructions and your desired level of crispness.

10. Coffee Waffles

Duration: 30 minutes

Yield: 12 waffles

Ingredient List

- Egg Replacer (2 tbsp.)
- Hot water (1/4 cup)
- Granulated sugar (3/4 cup)
- Baking powder (1 tsp.)
- Flour (1 ½ cups)
- Nutmeg (1/2 tsp.)
- Baking soda (1/2 tsp.)
- Salt (1/4 tsp.)
- Instant Coffee (2 tbsp.)
- Dairy-free soy margarine (1/2 cup, melted)
- Dairy-free soy yogurt (1/2 cup)
- Vanilla extract (1 tsp.)

HHHHHHHHHHHHHHHHHHHHHHHHHHHHH

How to Cook:

a) Combine all the ingredients listed in a large mixing bowl or a stand mixer.

b) Whisk the ingredients until fully combined and the mixture forms a smooth batter.

c) Let the batter rest for 10 minutes to allow it to thicken.

d) Preheat the waffle iron.

e) Pour 1/3 cup of the batter onto the waffle iron and spread it evenly.

f) Cook the waffle for about 4 minutes or until golden brown.

Cooking Notes:

a) Make sure the waffle iron is preheated to the recommended temperature before pouring the batter.

b) Use a measuring cup to ensure consistent waffle size.

c) Do not overfill the waffle iron with batter to avoid overflow.

11. Raisin and Oats Waffles

Duration: 30 minutes

Yield: 16 waffles

Ingredient List

- Flour (1 ½ cups)
- Almond milk (1 ½ cups)
- Raisins
- Baking powder (2 tsp.)
- Salt (1/2 tsp.)
- Granulated sugar (1 ¼ cup)
- Canola oil (1/2 cup)
- Baking soda (1/2 tsp.)
- Vanilla extract (1 tsp.)
- Hazelnut extract (1 tsp.)
- Oats (3/4 cup)
- Lemon Juice (2 tbsp.)

HHHHHHHHHHHHHHHHHHHHHHHHHHHHH

How to Cook:

a) Combine all the ingredients in a large mixing bowl or stand mixer.

b) Whisk until fully combined and the mixture forms a smooth batter.

c) Let the batter rest for 10 minutes.

d) Preheat the waffle iron.

e) Pour 1/3 cup of the batter onto the waffle iron and cook for 4 minutes.

f) Serve and enjoy!

Cooking Notes:

a) The batter may seem thin at first, but that's normal. It will thicken as it rests.

b) If you want your waffles to be crispier, leave them on the iron for a little longer.

c) To keep the waffles warm and crisp until serving, place them on a wire rack in a 200°F oven.

12. Strawberry Waffles

Duration: 40 minutes

Yield: 12 waffles

Ingredient List

- Flour (1 ¾ cups)
- Granulated sugar (1 cup)
- Baking soda (1 tsp.)
- Salt (1/4 tsp.)
- Strawberries (1 cup, mashed)
- Canola Oil (1/2 cup)
- White Distilled Vinegar (1 tbsp.)
- Vanilla extract (1 tsp.)

HHHHHHHHHHHHHHHHHHHHHHHHHHHH

How to Cook:

a) Combine all the ingredients in a large mixing bowl or stand mixer. Whisk until the mixture is fully combined and forms a smooth batter.

b) Let the batter rest for 10 minutes.

c) Preheat the waffle iron.

d) Pour 1/3 cup of the batter onto the iron and spread it evenly.

e) Cook the waffle for about 4 minutes or until golden brown.

f) Serve and enjoy with your favorite toppings like maple syrup, whipped cream, fresh berries, or chocolate chips.

Cooking Notes:

a) Make sure to preheat the waffle iron properly to avoid uneven cooking or sticking.

b) Avoid overmixing the batter as it can result in tough and dense waffles.

c) Adjust the cooking time according to the heat of your waffle iron and the desired crispness of the waffle.

d) If you don't have a waffle iron, you can use a griddle or non-stick pan to make pancake-like waffles.

13. Chocolate Chip Waffle

Yields: 12

Time Needed: 1 hour

Ingredient List

- Almond flour (2 cups)
- Arrowroot powder (1 tbsp.)
- Salt (1/ tsp.)
- Baking Soda (1/2 tsp.)
- Eggs (2)
- Honey (3 tbsp.)
- Coconut milk- full fat (1/2 cup)
- Vanilla (1 tsp.)
- Apple cider vinegar (2 tbsp.)
- Chocolate chips (1/2 cup, dark)

HHHHHHHHHHHHHHHHHHHHHHHHHHHHHH

How to Cook:

a) Combine all the ingredients in a large mixing bowl or a stand mixer.

b) Whisk the mixture until fully combined and it forms a smooth batter.

c) Let the batter rest for 10 minutes to allow it to thicken.

d) Preheat the waffle iron according to the manufacturer's instructions.

e) Pour 1/3 cup of the batter onto the preheated waffle iron.

f) Cook the waffle for 4-5 minutes or until golden brown.

Cooking Notes:

a) Make sure not to overmix the batter as it can result in tough waffles.

b) Resting the batter helps to allow the gluten to relax, resulting in fluffier waffles.

c) Adjust the cooking time according to the waffle iron and the desired level of crispiness.

14. Banana Waffles

Serves: 6

Cooking Time: 15 minutes

Ingredient List:

- 3 eggs
- 3 tbsp. melted butter,
- 1 cup whole-wheat flour
- 1 ½ cups milk
- 1 cup all-purpose flour
- 2 tsp. baking powder
- ½ tsp. salt
- 2 tbsp. honey
- 2 ripe bananas, sliced

HHHHHHHHHHHHHHHHHHHHHHHHHHHHH

Cooking Time:

a) Combine the flours, salt and baking powder in a bowl.

b) In a blender, combine the milk, honey, melted butter, and bananas.

c) Process the mixture in the blender until it becomes smooth.

d) Fold the banana mixture into the dry ingredients and continue to stir until smooth.

e) Let the batter rest for 10 minutes.

f) Preheat the waffle iron.

g) Pour 1/3 cup of the batter on the iron and cook for 4 minutes.

h) Serve and enjoy.

Cooking Notes:

a) You can add chopped nuts or chocolate chips to the batter for added texture and flavor.

b) When cooking the waffles, be sure not to overfill the iron with batter as it can overflow and make a mess.

c) Waffles can be kept warm in the oven on a low heat setting until ready to serve.

15. Lemon Waffles

Yield: 24

Total Cooking Time: 20 Minutes

Ingredient List

- Yellow waffles mix: 1 package
- Lemon-flavored gelatin: 1 package
- Vegetable oil: ¾ cup
- Eggs:4
- Water: ¾ cup
- Lemon extract: ¼ tsp
- Confectioner's Sugar: 1 cup
- Lemon juice: 4 tbsp.

HHHHHHHHHHHHHHHHHHHHHHHHHHHHHH

How to Cook:

a) In a mixing bowl, combine the flours, salt, and baking powder.

b) In a blender, add the milk, honey, melted butter, and bananas.

c) Process the mixture until it becomes smooth.

d) Fold the banana mixture into the dry ingredient mixture and continue stirring until it becomes smooth.

e) Let the batter rest for 10 minutes to allow the mixture to thicken and become more elastic.

f) Preheat the waffle iron.

g) Pour 1/3 cup of the batter onto the iron and cook it for 4 minutes or until the waffle turns golden brown.

h) Serve the waffles warm with your preferred toppings, such as whipped cream, maple syrup, or fresh fruits.

Cooking Notes:

a) Make sure to mix the dry ingredients well before adding the wet ingredients to ensure that everything is evenly distributed.

b) Letting the batter rest allows the gluten in the flour to relax, resulting in a fluffier waffle.

c) Adjust the cooking time and heat according to your waffle iron's instructions and your desired level of crispiness.

16. Blackberry waffles

Yield: 9

Total Cooking Time: 35 Minutes

Ingredient List

- Flour: 2 cups
- White sugar: 1 ½ cup
- Baking powder: 2 tsp
- Salt: 1 tsp
- Margarine: 2/3 cup
- Eggs: 2
- Milk: 2/3 cup
- Blueberries: 1 cup

HHHHHHHHHHHHHHHHHHHHHHHHHHHH

How to Cook:

a) In a mixing bowl, combine the flours, salt, and baking powder.

b) In a blender, combine the milk, honey, melted butter, and bananas.

c) Process the ingredients in the blender until smooth.

d) Fold the banana mixture into the dry ingredients in the mixing bowl, stirring until smooth.

e) Let the batter rest for 10 minutes to allow the ingredients to combine and create a smoother texture.

f) Preheat the waffle iron.

g) Pour 1/3 cup of the batter onto the waffle iron and cook for about 4 minutes or until the waffles are golden brown.

h) Serve warm and enjoy!

Cooking Notes:

a) Make sure to blend the wet ingredients well in the blender to ensure a smoother texture.

b) Letting the batter rest for a few minutes will allow the ingredients to combine, making the waffles fluffier.

c) Be careful not to overfill the waffle iron with batter, as it may spill over and make a mess.

d) These waffles go great with toppings such as sliced bananas, berries, whipped cream, or syrup.

17. Apple waffles

Yield: 12

Total Cooking Time: 60 Minutes

Ingredient List

- Flour: 3 cups
- White sugar: 2 cups
- Salt: 1 tsp
- Baking soda: 1 tsp
- Vegetable oil: 1 ¼ cup
- Vanilla extract: 2 tsp
- Eggs: 3
- Apples, peeled, chopped: 2 ½ cups
- Chopped walnuts: 1 cup
- Brown sugar: 1 ¼ cups
- Milk: 1/3 cup
- Butter, ½ cup

HHHHHHHHHHHHHHHHHHHHHHHHHHHHHH

How to Cook:

a) In a bowl, combine the flours, salt, and baking powder.

b) In a blender, combine the milk, honey, melted butter, and bananas.

c) Process the ingredients in the blender until smooth.

d) Fold the banana mixture into the dry ingredients and continue stirring until the batter is smooth.

e) Let the batter rest for 10 minutes.

f) Preheat the waffle iron.

g) Pour 1/3 cup of the batter onto the iron and cook for 4 minutes.

h) Serve and enjoy.

Cooking Notes: Make sure to blend the ingredients until the batter is completely smooth. Letting the batter rest for 10 minutes helps to create a lighter texture. Adjust the amount of batter you pour onto the waffle iron according to the manufacturer's instructions. Serve with your favorite toppings, such as fresh fruit, whipped cream, or maple syrup.

18. Almond Cherry Waffles

Yield: 6

Total Cooking Time: 1hr 10 Minutes

Ingredient List

- Butter, 8 tbsp.
- Flour: 1 cup
- Baking powder: ½ tsp
- Salt: ½ tsp
- Sugar: ¾ cup
- Eggs: 3
- Almond extract: ½ tsp
- Frozen cherries, drained and thawed: 12 oz.
- Sliced almonds: ½ cup

HHHHHHHHHHHHHHHHHHHHHHHHHHHHH

How to Cook:

a) In a mixing bowl, combine the flours, salt, and baking powder.

b) In a blender, combine the milk, honey, melted butter, and bananas. Process until smooth.

c) Fold the banana mixture into the dry ingredient list and continue stirring until the batter is smooth.

d) Allow the batter to rest for 10 minutes.

e) Preheat the waffle iron.

f) Pour 1/3 cup of the batter onto the waffle iron.

g) Cook for 4 minutes or until the waffles are golden brown.

h) Remove the waffles from the iron and serve them hot.

i) Enjoy your delicious banana waffles!

Cooking Notes:

a) Use ripe bananas for the best flavor and texture.

b) Be sure not to overmix the batter as it can make the waffles tough.

c) Adjust the cooking time according to the instructions of your waffle iron.

d) Serve with your favorite toppings like butter, maple syrup, whipped cream, or fresh fruits.

19. Lemon Ginger Waffles

Yield: 12

Total Cooking Time: 1hr 20 Minutes

Ingredient List

- Butter, 1 cup
- Flour: 3 cups
- Grated lemon zest: 2 tbsp. + 1/3 cup lemon juice
- Minced garlic: 1/3 cup
- Baking soda: 1 tsp
- Salt: 1 tsp
- Granulated sugar: 2 ½ cups
- Eggs: 6
- Sour cream: 1 cup
- Confectioner's sugar for dusting

HHHHHHHHHHHHHHHHHHHHHHHHHHHHHH

How to Cook:

a) Combine the flours, salt, and baking powder in a mixing bowl.

b) In a blender, add the milk, honey, melted butter, and bananas.

c) Process the ingredients until the mixture becomes smooth.

d) Fold the banana mixture into the dry ingredients and continue stirring until the batter becomes smooth.

e) Let the batter rest for 10 minutes to allow the ingredients to blend.

f) Preheat the waffle iron.

g) Pour 1/3 cup of the batter onto the waffle iron.

h) Cook the waffles for about 4 minutes or until they turn golden brown.

i) Serve and enjoy your freshly made banana waffles.

Cooking Notes: You can add other ingredients like chopped nuts, chocolate chips, or whipped cream to make the waffles more delicious. If the batter is too thick, you can add more milk to thin it out. The cooking time may vary depending on your waffle iron, so make sure to follow the instructions carefully.

20. Cinnamon Coffee Waffles

Yield: 6

Total Cooking Time: 55 Minutes

Ingredient List

- 2 cups Flour
- Sugar: ¾ cups
- 2 tbsp. Sugar (for Cinnamon Sugar)
- 1 tbsp. Baking powder
- Salt: ½ tsp
- ½ cup Vegetable shortening
- Cinnamon: 1 tsp
- Egg: 1
- Milk: ¾ cup
- Butter, 2 tbsp.

HHHHHHHHHHHHHHHHHHHHHHHHHHHH

How to Cook:

a) Combine all dry ingredients (flours, salt, and baking powder) in a bowl.

b) In a blender, combine milk, honey, melted butter, and bananas until smooth.

c) Fold the banana mixture into the dry ingredients and continue stirring until smooth.

d) Let the batter rest for 10 minutes.

e) Preheat the waffle iron.

f) Pour 1/3 cup of batter on the waffle iron and cook for 4 minutes.

g) Serve the waffle and enjoy.

Cooking Notes:

a) Make sure the banana mixture is fully blended before folding it into the dry ingredients.

b) Resting the batter for 10 minutes allows the baking powder to activate and results in fluffier waffles.

c) Adjust the cooking time based on the instructions of your waffle iron.

21. Plum waffles

Yield: 10

Total Cooking Time: 1 hr. 30 Minutes

Ingredient List

- Butter, ¾ cup
- Flour: 1 ½ cups + 2 tbsp.
- Baking soda: ½ tsp
- Salt: ¼ tsp
- Brown sugar: ½ cup
- Vanilla extract: 1 tsp
- Lemon zest: 2 tsp
- Sour cream: ¼ cup
- Plum, pitted, halved, and cut into 3
- Confectioner sugar for dusting

HHHHHHHHHHHHHHHHHHHHHHHHHHHHHH

How to Cook:

a) Combine the flours, salt, and baking powder in a bowl.

b) In a blender, blend milk, honey, melted butter, and bananas until smooth.

c) Fold the banana mixture into the dry ingredients and stir until smooth.

d) Let the batter rest for 10 minutes.

e) Preheat the waffle iron.

f) Pour 1/3 cup of the batter onto the waffle iron and cook for 4 minutes.

g) Serve and enjoy.

Cooking Notes:

a) Make sure to blend the wet ingredients until completely smooth before adding them to the dry ingredients.

b) Letting the batter rest for 10 minutes allows the ingredients to fully absorb into each other and creates a fluffier waffle.

c) Use a 1/3 measuring cup to ensure that the waffles are the same size and cook evenly.

22. Coconut Pineapple Waffles

Yield: 10

Total Cooking Time: 1 hr. 25 Minutes

Ingredient List

- Shredded coconut: 1 ½ cup
- Butter, ½ cup
- Flour: 1 ½ cups
- Baking soda: ½ tsp
- Salt: ½ tsp
- Sugar: 1 cup
- Eggs: 3
- Sour cream: 1 cup
- Pineapple chunks with juice: 1 can

HHHHHHHHHHHHHHHHHHHHHHHHHHHHHH

How to Cook:

a) In a mixing bowl, combine the flours, salt, and baking powder.

b) In a blender, add the milk, honey, melted butter, and bananas.

c) Process the mixture in the blender until smooth.

d) Pour the banana mix into the dry ingredient mixture and stir until smooth.

e) Let the batter rest for 10 minutes to allow the ingredients to meld together.

f) Preheat the waffle iron.

g) Pour 1/3 cup of the batter onto the waffle iron and cook for 4 minutes.

Cooking Notes:

a) Be careful not to overmix the batter as this may result in tough waffles.

b) It's important to let the batter rest for 10 minutes to allow the flour to absorb the liquid ingredients properly.

c) Adjust the amount of honey depending on how sweet you want your waffles to be.

d) Serve with your favorite toppings like fresh fruit, whipped cream, and maple syrup.

23. Walnut Honey Waffles

Yield: 10

Total Cooking Time: 1 hr. 20 Minutes

Ingredient List

- Walnuts, halved: 2 oz.
- Butter: 1 tsp
- Flour: 1 ½ cups
- Honey: 1 cup + 2 tbsp.
- Applesauce: 1 cup
- Eggs: 3
- Baking soda: ¾ cup
- Salt: 1 tsp
- Ground ginger: ¼ tsp

HHHHHHHHHHHHHHHHHHHHHHHHHHHHHH

How to Cook:

a) Combine the flours, salt and baking powder in a bowl.

b) In a blender, combine the milk, honey, melted butter, and bananas.

c) Process until smooth.

d) Fold the banana mix into the dry Ingredient List and continue stirring until smooth.

e) Let the batter rest for 10 minutes.

f) Preheat the waffle iron.

g) Pour 1/3 cup batter on the iron and cook for 4 minutes.

h) Serve and enjoy.

Cooking Notes:

a) For best results, make sure the battery is fully mixed and smooth.

b) Allowing the batter to rest for 10 minutes will help the waffles become more fluffy.

c) Preheat the waffle iron to avoid undercooked or unevenly cooked waffles.

d) Use a measuring cup to ensure even portions and cooking time.

e) Serve with toppings such as fresh fruit, whipped cream, or maple syrup.

24. Orange Cornmeal Waffles

Yield: 8

Total Cooking Time: 1hr 10 Minutes

Ingredient List

- Olive oil: ½ cup
- 2 large Eggs
- Sugar:1 cup
- 1/3 cup Sugar (for the top crust)
- ½ cup Orange juice
- Flour: 1 ¼ cup
- Yellow cornmeal: ½ cup
- Baking powder: 2 tsp
- Salt: 1 tsp
- Orange zest grated: 1

HHHHHHHHHHHHHHHHHHHHHHHHHHHH

How to Cook:

a) Combine the dry ingredients: In a mixing bowl, combine the flours, salt, and baking powder.

b) Blend the wet ingredients: In a blender, combine the milk, honey, melted butter, and bananas. Process until smooth.

c) Mix the batter: Fold the banana mixture into the dry ingredients and continue stirring until a smooth batter forms.

d) Rest the batter: Allow the batter to rest for 10 minutes.

e) Preheat the waffle iron: While the batter is resting, preheat the waffle iron.

f) Cook the waffles: Pour 1/3 cup of batter onto the waffle iron and cook for 4 minutes or until golden brown.

g) Serve and enjoy: Serve the waffles warm with your desired toppings such as maple syrup, whipped cream, or fresh fruits.

Cooking Notes:

a) For a fluffier texture, beat the egg whites separately until stiff peaks form and fold it into the batter before cooking.

b) Don't overmix the batter, as it can result in tough waffles.

c) Adjust the sweetness according to your preference by adding more or less honey.

d) Leftover waffles can be stored in an airtight container in the fridge for up to 3 days or in the freezer for up to 3 months. Reheat in the toaster or oven before serving.

25. Chocolate Waffles

Cooking Time: 30 minutes

Yield: 12 waffles

Ingredient List

- Coconut milk (1 cup)
- Sugar (3/4 cup)
- Canola oil (1/3 cup)
- Cider vinegar (1 ½ tsp.)
- Vanilla (extract-1 tsp.)
- All-purpose flour (1 cup)
- Cocoa powder (1/3 cup)
- Baking soda (3/4 tsp.)
- Baking powder (1/2 tsp.)
- Salt (1/4 tsp.)

HHHHHHHHHHHHHHHHHHHHHHHHHHHHHH

How to Cook:

a) In a bowl, mix the flours, salt, and baking powder.

b) In a blender, blend the milk, honey, melted butter, and bananas until smooth.

c) Add the banana mixture into the dry ingredient mixture and continue to stir until the batter is smooth.

d) Let the batter rest for 10 minutes to allow the gluten to relax and distribute the moisture.

e) Preheat the waffle iron to the desired temperature.

f) Pour 1/3 cup batter onto the waffle iron and cook for about 4 minutes, or until golden brown and crispy.

g) Remove the waffle from the iron and place it onto a plate.

h) Serve immediately with your desired toppings, and enjoy!

Cooking Notes:

a) You can use either a classic or Belgian waffle iron for this recipe, but note that the cooking time may vary between different types and brands of waffle irons.

b) Be sure to let the batter rest before cooking to ensure a tender and fluffy texture.

c) For best results, pour the batter onto the waffle iron in a gentle and even stream.

d) Customize your waffles with toppings like sliced bananas, berries, whipped cream, and maple syrup.

26. Pumpkin Waffles

Duration: 35 minutes

Yield: 12 waffles

Ingredient List

- Almond milk (1/4 cup)
- Cider vinegar (1 tsp.)
- All-purpose flour (1 ¼ cup)
- Baking soda (1/2 tsp.)
- Granulated sugar (1/3 cup)
- Brown sugar (1/3 cup)
- Baking powder (1 tsp.)
- Cashews (1/4 cup, ground finely)
- Cinnamon (1 tsp.)
- Ginger (1/2 tsp.)
- Nutmeg (1/2 tsp.)
- Salt (1/2 tsp.)
- Pumpkin (1/2 cup, pureed)
- Canola oil (1/3 cup)
- Sour cream (2 tsp., dairy free)
- Vanilla extract (1 tsp.)

HHHHHHHHHHHHHHHHHHHHHHHHHHHHHH

How to Cook:

a) Preheat the oven to 350° F.

b) In a small bowl, mix vinegar and almond milk together and set aside for 5 minutes.

c) In a large bowl, mix baking powder, flour, baking soda, cinnamon, cashews, nutmeg, ginger, and salt together.

d) In another bowl, mix canola oil, pumpkin puree, vanilla, sour cream, and vinegar mixture together.

e) Add the liquid mixture to the dry Ingredient List and combine until everything is evenly distributed.

f) Line the muffin tin with paper liners and fill each mold about 2/3 full with batter.

g) Bake for 20 minutes or until a toothpick inserted in the center comes out clean.

h) Remove from heat and allow to cool before topping with the desired frosting.

Cooking Notes:

a) Make sure the almond milk and vinegar mixture has been set aside for at least 5 minutes before using it in the recipe.

b) When mixing the dry ingredients together, ensure there are no lumps in the mixture.

c) Use an ice cream scoop or measuring cup to ensure uniformity when filling the muffin molds.

d) Allow the muffins to cool before adding any frosting to prevent melting.

27. French Vanilla Waffles

Duration: 30 minutes

Yield: 16 waffles

Ingredient List

- Almond milk (1 ½ cups)
- Lemon juice (1 tsp.)
- Flour (2 ¼ cups)
- Baking powder (2 tsp.)
- Baking soda (1/2 tsp.)
- Salt (1/2 tsp.)
- Granulated sugar (1 ¼ cup)
- Canola oil (1/2 cup)
- Vanilla extract (1 tsp.)
- Hazelnut extract (1 tsp.)

HHHHHHHHHHHHHHHHHHHHHHHHHHHHH

How to Cook:

a) In a mixing bowl, combine the flours, salt and baking powder.

b) In a blender, combine the milk, honey, melted butter, and bananas. Process until smooth.

c) Fold the banana mixture into the dry ingredients and continue stirring until smooth.

d) Let the batter rest for 10 minutes.

e) Preheat the waffle iron.

f) Pour 1/3 cup batter on the waffle iron and cook for 4 minutes or until golden brown.

g) Serve the waffles immediately, garnish with your favorite toppings, and enjoy.

Cooking Notes:

a) Make sure to measure the flour correctly using the spoon and level method to avoid adding too much flour and making the waffles dense.

b) Be sure not to overmix the batter, as it can result in tough waffles.

c) To keep the waffles warm while cooking in batches, place them on a wire rack on a baking sheet in a 200°F oven.

d) Experiment with different toppings such as fresh fruit, whipped cream, chocolate chips, or maple syrup to add more flavor and texture to your waffles.

28. Vegan White Waffles

Cooking Time: 30 minutes

Yield: 12 waffles

Ingredient List

- Dairy free soy margarine (3/4 cups, softened)
- Granulated sugar (1 ½ cups)
- Soy yogurt vanilla (1/4 cup)
- Vanilla (2 tsp.)
- Silken tofu (1/4 cup, pureed)
- All-purpose flour (2 cups)
- Baking powder (1 tsp.)
- Salt (1 tsp.)
- Coconut milk (1 cup)

HHHHHHHHHHHHHHHHHHHHHHHHHHHHHH

How to Cook:

a) Combine the flours, salt and baking powder in a large mixing bowl.

b) In a blender, add the milk, honey, melted butter, and bananas, and process until smooth.

c) Fold the banana mixture into the dry ingredients in the mixing bowl, and continue stirring until smooth.

d) Let the batter rest for 10 minutes to allow the ingredients to meld together.

e) Preheat the waffle iron to the desired temperature.

f) Using a measuring cup or ladle, pour 1/3 cup of batter onto the waffle iron and cook for 4 minutes or until golden brown.

g) Remove the waffle from the iron and place on a plate.

h) Serve with your favorite toppings such as butter, syrup, whipped cream, and sliced bananas.

Cooking Notes:

a) For a crispy waffle exterior, you can lightly spray the waffle iron with cooking spray before pouring the batter.

b) Be careful not to overmix the batter, as this can result in tough waffles. Mix only until the ingredients are fully combined.

c) You can keep cooked waffles warm in a low oven until ready to serve.

d) To make ahead, you can freeze the cooked waffles in an airtight container and reheat them in a toaster or oven when ready to eat.

29. Mixed Nuts Waffles

Duration: 30 minutes

Yield: 12 waffles

Ingredient List

- Flour (1 ½ cup)
- Baking soda (1 tsp.)
- Ginger (1 tsp, ground)
- Cinnamon (1 tsp.)
- Nutmeg (1/4 tsp)
- Salt (1/2 tsp.)
- Granulated sugar (1 ¼ cup)
- Brown Sugar (1/3 cup)
- Baking powder (1/2 tsp.)
- Canola oil (1/2 cup)
- Soy yogurt (2 tsp., vanilla)
- Vanilla (1 tsp.)
- Cashews (1 cup, crushed)
- Hazelnuts (1/2 cup, crushed)
- Walnuts (1 cup, chopped)

HHHHHHHHHHHHHHHHHHHHHHHHHHHHHH

How to Cook:

a) In a mixing bowl, combine the flours, salt, and baking powder.

b) In a blender, combine the milk, honey, melted butter, and bananas. Process until smooth.

c) Fold the banana mixture into the dry ingredients and continue stirring until the batter is smooth.

d) Let the batter rest for 10 minutes to allow the ingredients to meld together.

e) Preheat your waffle iron to the desired temperature.

f) Grease the iron with cooking spray or melted butter.

g) Pour 1/3 cup of the batter onto the hot iron and cook for 3-5 minutes, or until golden brown.

h) Serve the waffles with your favorite toppings, such as butter, syrup, or fresh fruit.

Cooking Notes:

a) Over Mixing the batter can lead to tough and dense waffles. Be careful not to overmix!

b) If you prefer crispy waffles, use a higher temperature setting on your waffle iron and cook for slightly longer.

c) Leftover waffles can be stored in an airtight container in the fridge or freezer for later use. Reheat in a toaster or oven for best results.

Afterword's

Wow, what an incredible experience this has been. I couldn't have done it without your support and participation. As an author, I can only write the words, but it's up to the reader to bring them to life. And you did exactly that. You purchased this book, dedicated your time to reading it, and reached the end with me. I am deeply humbled.

While you've already done so much, I have one more request. I value feedback from my readers and would love to hear your thoughts on the book. I would be grateful if you could leave a review on Amazon. Not only will I see it, but it will also give others the opportunity to discover the book as well. The book community is a special one, and by sharing your thoughts, you are contributing to its growth and success.

Thank you for being so awesome.

Samantha Rich

Made in the USA
Middletown, DE
29 October 2023

41584226R10053